What Comes, What Goes

What Comes, What Goes

Poems by

Christopher Woods

© 2021 Christopher Woods. All rights reserved.
This material may not be reproduced in any form, published,
reprinted, recorded, performed, broadcast,
rewritten or redistributed without
the explicit permission of Christopher Woods.
All such actions are strictly prohibited by law.

Cover design by Shay Culligan

ISBN: 978-1-63980-022-3

Kelsay Books
502 South 1040 East, A-119
American Fork, Utah 84003
Kelsaybooks.com

For Linda, always

Acknowledgments

GREY WOLFE PRESS: "Porch Guardian"
BURNING WORLD LITERARY JOURNAL: "Party Favors"
VOICES DE LA LUNA: "Make Room! Make Room!"
POEM: "Divers"
EMPIRICAL: "Submarine"
POPPY ROAD REVIEW: "The Poet Goes Home"
34 ORCHARD: "The Reader"
PUDDING: "Books in a Box"
NEW VERSE NEWS: "Cigar Store Indian"
COMMUTER LIT: "Up On That Damp Bed"
ZONE 3: "Boneyard Elegy"
RIO GRANDE REVIEW; and *INSCAPE:* "Hardwood Floor"
THE YALE REVIEW FOR THE HUMANITIES IN MEDICINE:
　　"Ghosts in Gowns"

Contents

Tennessee	13
Post Estrangment	15
Aperture	16
In the Old Days	17
It was the season of great birds	18
Leaving Manhattan by Bus	19
Not Forgetting	20
Porch Guardian	21
Party Favors	22
Roadside Shrines	24
For The Union Dead, Hempstead, Texas	25
Make Room! Make Room!	26
Visit to the Old Convent on Almeda Road	27
Divers	29
Submarine	31
The Farmer's Wife	32
Brooklyns	33
Books in a Box	34
the reader	35
The Poet Goes Home	37
The Winter People	38
Cigar Store Indian	39
Up On That Damp Bed	40
Boneyard Elegy	41
Hardwood Floor	43
Ghosts in Gowns	44

"My! People come and go so quickly here!"
—*The Wizard of Oz*

Tennessee

Outside Pigeon Forge, the highway mists
In waning dusk.
My hands and eyes aching, I pull to the side
To rest,
To dream it all again, in sequence.

Walking through underbrush,
Smoky Mountain air lures me to the past.
In my jacket, I carry arrowheads,
Ones you left.
You left them, not for me, just left them.
A man leaves hints of what he was.
Arrowheads, cool and sharp, are all I have of you.

I must have been clouds then, when you lived.
Dressed in flannels, you Geiger-counted the hills,
To take Tennessee if you could,
As it has always been in family lore.
Your journeys were holy travels, personal crusades.

Brother in time, we are tantamount to seasons
Of unbroken circles.
It all depends where and how time places itself.
Grandfather, I never even met you.
Time is dead but for the living,
So how to annihilate time
And get to know each other outside the concept
Intrigues me.

As for you, old man, this vision will last,
Flickering in photographic haze.
Do you want to know something?
No matter how I stand
Mine is still a Neanderthal walk,
Clutching these arrowheads in Tennessee?

Post Estrangment

The man who owned that land
Told us to look away from the mound.
A flint maker worked away from fire and smoke, he told us.

So southwest from the mound we set to work.
Dug delicately in wild brush, in the soil.
We looked for arrowheads, flints
Indians had left behind.

We scoured an old crusty riverbed.
Found brachiopods and took them as loot.
Later, kneeling at the mound, our fingers cut and dirty,
I realized something.
This was the first thing we had really done together in months.

Aperture

They line up as he has asked,
Twelve innocent corn fed kids
For their senior class photograph
In a disappearing Nebraska town.
They smile on command,
And this is what he wants
To escape, to somehow forget.

It must be the new camera.
Each time he trains it
On the unsuspecting young,
He sees their futures.

Today, he sees
A woman who dies in childbirth,
One in a fatal car wreck,
Another from a bad heart.
Two are condemned to long,
Loveless marriages.
The others, the fortunate, will live well.
One, who will outlive them all,
Will celebrate one hundred years,
But every night she will dream
Of her high school boyfriend
Who moved away to Georgia
To love another man.

In the Old Days

We travelled by foot,
horse and wagon,
waiting for a promise
of great machines
to deliver us
into the future.

The machines came,
so many of them
with problems
and a high price.
air turned foul
and the sky unnatural.

Long ago,
when I was a kid,
we watched the ghost trains
carry the last of the dinosaurs.
They passed through our town
once a year or so.

Now the trains roll on through
empty towns and cities
carry relics of humans
no one is left
alive to see.

It was the season of great birds

Crashing to the ground outside our windows
And on the roof, leaving holes for the empty
Clouds that floated gently into the rooms,
Landing on our heads and the floor.

No rain, no rain, the ground cracking,
The wells gone dry,
Watched as the last blue crane swooped
So desperately low and close that its sad eyes
Met our own before it expired on the walkway
Out the back door.

Already we had been inside for weeks
Fearing going outside, becoming sun victims
Or killed by falling birds and clouds.
Now, as the dry darkness envelops the world,
We pass our last jug of water between us,
Savoring it, the very life of it.

Leaving Manhattan by Bus

Pennsylvania passes by
a steady blur
for her, so weary
after five months in the city
dreaming of home
but afraid to go back,
standing nightly
in Times Square,
crossroads of the world.
she has known
thousands of hands and tongues,
learned how to get by
without being killed.

Now the hills and pastures
are a softer ride
for her and the baby
beginning to dream
deep inside her.
She will tell you
there are no mistakes,
no coincidences.

She likes the countryside,
fewer people, no bickering.
She dreams too,
of Las Vegas,
where her bus ticket expires,
where she is told
the people are kind.

Not Forgetting

Memory still a guide
in some ways,
his hands glide
over new folds, moles,
old injuries, everything
a body wears over time

Yet he remembers her
as she was, sixty years
ago when he too was young
and still with sight
like old pictures
that stay, stay, stay
hang in the head

But now those photographs
are blind too, meaningless
little cuts of paper he shuffles
like his days and nights

And on this special day
as he waits for the hearse
that will take her away
further into darkness,
from his touch
that won't forget
how blue cold
she has become.

Porch Guardian

The old house as you left it,
the rocker, the door that takes you
into the past, forty, maybe fifty
years ago,
and magically, the old dog,
always the patient friend,
still there,
waiting to greet you,
as if you never left
at all.

Party Favors

He passes the old place daily,
The abandoned mill where his grandfather
Worked, made his livelihood
And sense of his life, making wood
Products, until the job went elsewhere.

He thinks about the old man now,
Several times a day sometimes.
His own father checked out early,
Disappeared, followed a dream
That didn't include family.
His grandfather took him in,
Raised him best he could.
Good years, no matter what,
No one could take that away.

Now, his grandfather dead,
He's on his own at thirty-eight,
On the road five days a week,
Selling party favors, cheap trinkets
Made in Thailand and China.
Party hats and blowers, confetti,
Candles that won't blow out,
Napkins and plates with clown motifs.
Crap, every last bit of it,
All made by little kids worked numb,
Who never wear party hats.
He passes the old mill now.
He's popping pills to stay awake,
Other pills to stay sane and numb.
He rolls down the window to smell

The field, the creek, the old mill,
He wants to scream but he's too tired.
He's already late for his appointments.
Venders depend on him, his party favors.
Many celebrations await.

Roadside Shrines

for a child in diapers wandering
the wife escaping the house of bruises
old man wandering off to die alone
kids drunk on vodka on their way to the prom
all moving on and beyond all this

unsure my final destination
I drive toward the next town,
the doubts and possibilities,
eighty miles an hour

see the faded artificial roses
full moon white cross
so quickly,
a glance is all

am reminded how things can go.

For The Union Dead, Hempstead, Texas

Some mornings, fog shrouds the world
both above and below ground
so that time and war are hidden.

Not far away, a woman cooks grits
listens to a train whistle that lures her
far from the white frame house
where her husband sleeps.

You too are sleeping, still, dozens of you
Yankee boys who came south to fight,
who never went home.
As if being captured, kept in a POW camp
wasn't enough,
the gods of war had more ominous plans.

Yellow fever took no prisoners,
and one by one you fell from grace,
hundreds sick, soon to die.

Fog of war, of old conflict,
makes the world disappear.
Cows, dark hulks of dawn,
now grace this wide pasture.
Even the crude cedar crosses
that once marked your graves
now a memory no one remembers.

Make Room! Make Room!

Their field is wide
Enough for the soldiers
From every country in time.

Crowded, always crowded,
Not an inch to turn
Away from so much grief.
But still the god calls to them,
"Make room! Make room!"

And so they bunch closer
Together, a Roman soldier,
A Viet Cong boy in black,
Doughboys without faces,
Grudgingly make room
For the new war dead
Arriving unexpectedly
At all dark, bloody hours.

Death's badges identify them
Victims of catapults, boiling oil,
I.E.D.s, napalm and gas,
Sticks and stones,
All the tools of the wars
That led them all here
Where there is no need
To speak, only to acknowledge
Tears and every once proud flag.

Visit to the Old Convent on Almeda Road

Walking these grounds
Forty years later,
All seems pristine.
But there was also then.

New saplings around us, then.
There was music, a minuet.
Maria Chapala and I
Danced in powdered wigs
And flimsy blue costumes
Painstakingly sewn by our mothers.
We did our pubescent best
In a contest we did not win.

Now the trees are huge,
Old water oaks with healthy leaves.
But I notice they have grown crooked.
They stagger across their small earth,
Lean this way and that.
They are like the nuns
Assigned here early on,
Before lives and loins might heat.
Girls too young to know
Of lovers, possibilities.
Denied in their only youth,
They might have known touch,
The feel of another's body.

Now the trees even obscure
The very view of the convent,
Where women, prematurely old,

Hide inside their robes
Shrouded from the sun.
They are secrets,
Even to themselves.

Divers

In wetsuits they smoke and clown
At the river's edge,
Wishing they were still asleep.
They dance to shake the chill,
To stave off the sadness
Of their inevitable rescue.
At midnight they don masks and fins,
Waddle into the river,
Never to emerge the same again.

Night seals the river like a shroud.
Volunteer car lights pierce the dark flow.
Murky water, coffee colored,
Hides the missing from them.
But the divers plunge into the river
To retrieve missing parts of themselves,
Of all of us.
They dodge bites of fish
In a wavering ghost light
That comes and goes from shore.

A foot misplaced, a call unheard,
Anything can drown a man.
His lungs ready to burst,
He reclines in the fluid darkness,
The river's wet womb enclosing him.
He glides dreamily across sandbars,
Grazed by gar and catfish,
Drifting, forgetting songs and faces.
For blue lungs, their lights extinguished,
Life becomes a hum of rapids.

Divers reach out for the lost,
But the river is thick, filled with mud,
Teeming with phantom arms and legs
That appear only to evaporate.
Yet from experience they know
That by dawn the treasure arrives.
Perhaps clenched by weeds at the shore
Or floating free on the calm morning flow.
A man arrives, still dancing
In a river, in a story, that never ends.

Submarine

Open to the public for the weekend,
my father and I go to take the tour.
The mammoth hulk of a thing awaits,
men in their sailor whites at attention,
the day brilliant as we leave the deck
venture below where the nuclear
organs of this deep diving machine wait
in silence for the order, the moment
for which they have been created.

My father, working with one lung,
sees the ladder we must descend.
If he thinks it might be difficult
for him to manage those rungs,
he does not say.
I say, go first, take your time.

I watch his careful descent
as he disappears below me.
I think of things leaving,
how the sub will soon
leave the dock for duty,
plunge into the wet deepness
of dark nothing we will never see.
But I know there are all kinds of nothing.
I grab the top rungs, begin my own
descent into the sub, the sea,
and, soon, life without my father
going first.

The Farmer's Wife

Nights are her freedom.
After sunset the dreams stir
As she washes the dishes,
Puts the babies to bed.
When the last lights are out,
She climbs into bed beside him,
His rough hands, three day beard,
Her husband of six years,
Listens to his exhausted sleep.

Her magic show begins.
The old lovers come one by one,
Surround the bed, gesturing,
Begging her to return to them.
She welcomes each one,
None of them yet twenty,
Their touch, their taste, their glory
Still not faded in her mind
Most nights, the darkness swollen,
Pregnant with meaning,
Until she is spent, exhausted.

When daylight comes, she awakens
In a stale bed, a vacant life,
Every morning so much like the next.

Brooklyns

Many years later
As she waits
For her third husband
To come home,
Suspecting he will not,

She hears the wind
Pound the windows
Sees it sway the trees
Feels a chill in the room

Remembers something
Forgotten since childhood
When she and a neighbor boy
Came across a gypsy woman
Playing violin on the sidewalk,
A song so long ago
In Brooklyn.

It comes to her now
How sad that song was
So hopeless
It seemed to a child
On her way for candy
But instead found the gypsy.

How, as years drone on,
Some songs never change.

Books in a Box

A friend told me this.
Another told him.
It started back of that.
Someone happened on a box
In a used bookstore.
A box of books,
Sitting there, waiting.
They had belonged to someone,
A poet who had died.
He was gone,
But there were his books.
Other people's books, signed,
Dedicated to this poet that died
Not so naturally
As bitterly early.

Soon word got around.
Others went to that store
To see the books.
No one bought them.
Someone said, how could his wife
Have done this, let the books go?
The answer was this,
That she wanted a clean slate.
She didn't want his books
If she couldn't have him.

But she does, still.
He comes back to her,
To us all in fact.
Line by line.
Sometimes a random phrase,
Something out of sequence,
Something growing old now.

the reader

we heard he was coming
weeks before, when people
in the village heard from relatives
the other side of the east mountain.

we lined up, some against
our will, our hands open
to promise or doom
by lines sketched in our palms.

to be judged
was worrisome, even frightening.
but people came to the town square,
children hiding behind mothers' skirts,
husbands stern and resolute,
ready to be appraised.

but when the man
began to look at our hands
outstretched, some shaking,
he began to cry.
he said nothing, offered no advice,
only looked at hand after hand,
large and small, and wept
as the lines began to grow,
one hand to the next,
stringing us together
until we were all connected,
inseparable, joined in a web
of whatever bound us together.

not looking at each other,
afraid to move,
we watched the reader
as he left our village,
heading toward the west mountain,
where the next village waited
for his arrival.

The Poet Goes Home

The train is on time, and you appreciate this even as you understand the irony of it. Soon you will be there again. Home.

A bridge, the blue hills, a forest, open fields beneath the deep sky, smell of salt sea air—all talismans of home, of youth, of memory itself. How many times have you ridden these same rails, in all kinds of emotional weather?

Going away to the military academy, coming home for the holidays, going to the city for university, riding home with friends for your wedding, leaving with your new bride for the honeymoon, coming home a few years later dejected and alone, or when setting out again to live overseas, and finding a new life for yourself, coming close to marrying again, deciding against it, taking another train to the Far East while you decided about matters of faith, falling ill in a desert country, becoming so sick you could not be moved, the final hours of fever and longing for home, and now the last return trip, over the inward sea of things familiar, the green fields guiding the train so gently, and then so slowly as the train enters the station, where those who will survive you wait to carry your casket to the cemetery where, as a youth, you once wrote poems about everything yet to come.

The Winter People

come from nowhere, when the leaves on the trees are gone, and, suddenly, there are houses that were not there before, when children you have never seen in the village play in the barren fields, how, late at night, women can be seen in windows, crossing rooms, and men dissolve into darkness when they turn off the lights, and I wonder who these people are, those who do not exist all year long until winter, when they enter our landscape, these we have never known, these we fear knowing because somehow they are not like the rest of us, winter after winter, when the land is asleep and they live for just a short time, only for the bleak months, before they steal away again.

The rest of us go on, go on. Four seasons. No escape.

Cigar Store Indian

Late afternoon wind
gathers the scratch-off tickets
in the Quick-Stop parking lot
and makes tiny cyclones
around my headdress.
teenagers are barfing
cheap wine at my feet.
and yes, some people
do actually buy cigars here.

Don't ask me about before,
endless fields and streams,
wind blowing the high grasses
before the Iron Horse
and the cavalry arrived
with their diseases
and smallpox blankets
for trade.

Up On That Damp Bed

Some nights in a storm
when there's no money
to fix the roof

Or soaked with fever dreams
and visions known only to Blake
or the meth man up the street

Or crying a river
over the loss of one thing
or another that breaks the world

Or the baby coming early, too early

Or the river rising all around
the dark room in the night

Or incontinence that visits
so cruelly in later years

At least we can be thankful
for one thing, that soon enough
the bed will shift and shudder
and begin to float away
into a calm morning
elsewhere.

Boneyard Elegy

It was there for the taking,
Filled with victory
Or countless ways
Of being dominoed.
Early on, Nana pretended
She had to go there often
To replenish aces, deuces,
Whatever she had in short supply.
Later, when I played well,
She would send me there.
We became ruthless,
Always sending the other.

Once, when I was winning
And she waited for her turn,
She eyed the boneyard strangely,
Maybe remembering something, or someone.
Her face was without expression,
Or maybe filled with one
I was too young to understand.
She had to go there, but only once.
With that domino she won the round.

Sometimes I must still go there
For aces, deuces,
Whatever I have in short supply.
But even before I can touch them,
Dominoes seems to come to me.
It's Nana, I know,
Pushing them my way.
Still ruthless, she hands me fives,

Sixes, all the numbers I do not need.
Silent player, she lets me know
How there are no final hands,
Only hands that last and last.

Hardwood Floor

My dead grandmother
Was carried out of the house
But the wood still sang.

When Vietnam called
My soldier brother
Hesitated before going,
Found time to
Push me down the stairs,
Try to strangle me
Because I was reading
Books by Chairman Mao.
The floor remembers.

Later when my father lay dying
In celebration and in dirge,
A family possibly ending,
The floor knew and guided us.

This is how a house lives
Beyond namesake or the people
Who wander its veins.
This is how wood lives,
Remembering the forest,
A step here and there,
Across a floor,
In a clearing.

Ghosts in Gowns

They are coming
From the other end of the long hall
Where darkness huddles

Always coming in this direction
Toward the light that illuminates
Their gowns, pale skin, IV holders,
Even their invisible footprints
Across the hard linoleum sea

See how their gait falters,
Then grows stronger again
As darkness fades
And light itself offers a way

Until at last their gowns turn golden
And they are standing at the edge
Of this world
Ready to go on

About the Author

Christopher Woods is a writer and photographer who lives in Chappell Hill, Texas. His writing has appeared in hundreds of journals including *The Southern Review, New England Review/Bread Loaf Quarterly,* and *Glimmer Train.*

He has published a novel, *The Dream Patch,* a prose collection, *Under a Riverbed Sky,* and a book of stage monologues for actors, *Heart Speak.*

His photography prompt book for writers, *From Vision To Text,* is forthcoming from Propertius Press. His novella, *Hearts in the Dark,* was recently published by Running Wild Press. He has received residencies from The Ucross Foundation and the Edward Albee Foundation.

~

His photographs can be seen in his galleries:
instagram.com/dreamwood77019 and
christopherwoods.zenfolio.com

Made in the USA
Coppell, TX
27 September 2021